UPSIDE DOWN LIVING

sharing faith stories

[
The Upside-Down Living series emphasizes living out
one's Christian faith through the lens of Jesus
by following values that seem so countercultural
they appear to be upside down.
]

April Yamasaki

 **Herald Press**
Harrisonburg, Virginia

Upside-Down Living
Sharing Faith Stories

© 2017 by Herald Press, Harrisonburg, Virginia 22802. 800-245-7894.
All rights reserved.
International Standard Book Number: 978-1-5138-0172-8
Printed in United States of America

Written by April Yamasaki
Design by Merrill Miller
Cover photo by rez-art/iStockphoto/Thinkstock

Unless otherwise noted, Scripture text is quoted, with permission,
from the *New Revised Standard Version,* © 1989, Division of Christian
Education of the National Council of Churches of Christ in the United
States of America.

Some Scripture taken from *The Message.* © 2002. Used by permission
of NavPress Publishing Group.

20 19 18 17   10 9 8 7 6 5 4 3 2 1

Contents

Introduction 5

1. The Power of Story 7

2. Sharing Your Personal Story 13

3. Sharing Faith Stories for Every Day 19

4. Sharing Faith Stories in Words and Actions . . 25

5. Sharing Faith Stories When It's Difficult 31

6. Sharing Faith Stories as a Community. 37

About the Writer 43

[Introduction]

"It is significant that God does not present us with salvation in the form of an abstract truth, or a precise definition or a catchy slogan, but as *story*. . . . Story is an invitation to participate, first through our imagination and then, if we will, by faith—with our total lives in response to God."[1]

As we respond in faith with our whole lives, we join God's story. What better way, then, to share faith with others than by sharing faith stories that invite people to participate with us?

The possibilities are endless for sharing Bible stories, personal testimonies, stories from church history, and everyday anecdotes of faith in daily life. They can be shared in churches, at home, on the street, to children, youth, adults young and old, men and women, and everyone, "when you are at home and when you are away, when you lie down and when you rise" (Deuteronomy 6:7).

This six-session Bible study begins with the power of story, and then focuses on sharing your personal faith story in a variety of ways and settings—in church and in everyday life, in words and

---

1 Eugene H. Peterson, *The Message Remix: The Bible in Contemporary Language* (Carol Stream, IL: NavPress, 2003), 115.

actions, when sharing may be difficult, and when sharing as a faith community.

Each session includes biblical reflection, practical ideas, and questions for discussion and reflection that may also be used for journaling, action, and prayer. As I have prayed over and worked on these sessions, my hope is that they would inspire you to explore God's story and your own story more deeply and that what you discover would in turn inspire you to share with others.

Thank you for your part in God's story, and thank you to those readers who contributed ideas and questions. We share God's story—may we also share our faith stories with others.

—April Yamasaki

[1: The Power of Story]

"Do you know where your grandparents grew up? Do you know where your mom and dad went to high school? Do you know where your parents met?"[1] When psychologists asked children these and other related questions, they found that the children who knew more of their family story also proved to be the most self-confident and the most able to deal with stress. On the basis of this study, they concluded that stories function to give children a sense of belonging to something bigger than themselves and so contribute positively to their emotional health.

---

1   Bruce Feiler, "The Stories That Bind Us," *New York Times*, March 15, 2013, http://www.nytimes.com/2013/03/17/fashion/the-family-stories-that-bind-us-this-life.html.

In a similar way, sharing faith stories reminds us that we belong to a family of faith that is bigger than ourselves. The more we retell faith stories, the more we build identity and connection with one another, the more we nurture healthy faith and teach the younger generation, the more we build community and unity in the church. What's more, sharing faith stories can reach out to others beyond the church, building bridges of authentic relationship and extending an invitation of friendship and faith.

> Sharing faith stories is essential for both the in-reach of community building and the outreach of evangelism.

When I'm speaking to groups, I often begin with a story, or in the course of a sermon, I might illustrate a point with a personal anecdote. I notice that people tend to perk up at those times. A child looks up from her coloring book. A youth nudges his friend sitting next to him. A man three rows from the back leans forward on his elbows. A woman talks to me in the foyer afterward about something similar that happened to her. That's the power of story to build connections, and often it's the stories that people remember most.

One Friday afternoon, two young women came to my church and asked if they could see inside. Both were visiting from India, and they were so excited because they had never been inside a church before. They loved the red carpet, they loved the pews, they loved how big the sanctuary looked. And then one of them said, "But we have a question. Can you tell us the story of Jesus?"

> They wanted to hear a faith story—and not just any faith story, but the central story of Jesus.

So I told them that we believe that God came to us in Jesus. That in his life, death, and resurrection, Jesus shows us who God is and calls us to follow him in the way we live. Through his death on the cross and rising to new life, we have forgiveness from sin and the power to live a new life. Through God's Spirit with us today, we can be transformed; we can have hope even when life seems hard, because we have hope in God through Jesus Christ.

Not every faith story retells the story of Jesus in exactly this way. A faith story might share a personal testimony of how you came to know Jesus. Or a slice of life that gives a glimpse of God's Spirit at work to inspire, convict, forgive, or comfort. It might be a story of God's ongoing love and presence. Or a simple offer to pray for someone who's going through a hard time. In just a few words or a longer conversation, faith stories affirm God's activity in our own lives and in the world.

So if we're feeling shy, if we're not comfortable talking about ourselves, we don't need to worry, because the story of faith we share isn't mainly about ourselves. It's God's story written in our lives, and ultimately it's the story of Jesus, "the pioneer and perfecter of our faith" (Hebrews 12:2).

> Instead of making ourselves the center of attention, faith stories point to Jesus. Instead of being overwhelmed, we can be encouraged that Jesus has gone before us and now walks with us.

In his earthly ministry, Jesus told a lot of stories. Some were short parables about everyday objects that illustrated a spiritual point—like his story comparing the kingdom of God to a mustard tree (Matthew 13:31-32), or the even shorter story comparing God's kingdom to yeast that leavened a batch of bread (Matthew 13:33). Others were longer, like the story of the good Samaritan (Luke 10:30-37), and some included additional commentary, like the parable of the sower and the interpretation that follows (Mark 4:1-20).

The gospels recount Jesus' life in story form—like the story of his birth (Matthew 1:18-25; Luke 2:1-20), his meeting with the woman at the well who became one of the first evangelists (John 4:1-42), how he gave sight to a man who had been born blind (John 9:1-41), his painful arrest and death (Matthew 26:47–27:56; Mark 14:43–15:41; Luke 22:47–23:49; John 18:1–19:37), and his glorious resurrection (Matthew 28:1-10; Luke 24:1-12; John 20:1-29).

JOY DUNN KEENAN/MENNOMEDIA

> **The majority of the Bible consists of narrative, and more broadly, the entire Bible may be understood as God's story.**

In Scripture, God's people are encouraged to remember and retell faith stories to their children in the course of daily living (Deuteronomy 6:4-9; 20-25), to teach the next generation so that "they should set their hope in God, and not forget the works of God" (Psalm 78:7). Early Christians shared faith stories to spread the good news of Jesus (John 20:31; Acts 2:1-36). As we share faith stories today, we continue that legacy. So let us do so with joy and authenticity, with faith and courage, knowing that Jesus goes before us and is with us "always, to the end of the age" (Matthew 28:20).

[Talk about It]

▶ What biblical story has been significant in nurturing your faith? When did you first hear or read it? How has it shaped you?

▶ Not long ago I learned a new acronym, IRL, which stands for "in real life." It means not on the Internet, and not acted out in a movie or TV show, but in real life with people whom we know personally. What faith stories IRL have influenced you? Think of a parent, mentor, teacher, friend, or someone else whom you know personally. In what ways did they share their faith story with you?

▶ Think of the last time you shared a story with someone else— for example, recounting the events of the day to a loved one, reading a story to your children, sharing a funny story with someone at work, telling a Bible story in Sunday school, or sharing some other story. What did that story, and the way you told it, say about your faith, either in an overt manner or more subtly?

▶ One of the faith stories shared by Jesus appears in Luke 15:11-32. It's sometimes called "The Prodigal Son" (*NASB*), "The Parable of the Lost Son" (*NIV*), or "The Parable of the Prodigal and His Brother" (*NRSV*), but it could just as well be called "The Prodigal Father" because of the father's extravagant love, or in a more matter-of-fact way, "The Father and His Two Sons." All three play key roles in the story. Read the text, and consider what each character adds to the story. Which character most nearly reflects your life situation? In what ways does the portrayal of that character challenge you? What does the story as a whole reveal about who God is? What does it teach about responding to God in faith?

2:

[Sharing Your Personal Story]

For our call to worship last Christmas Eve, we chose a video of children retelling and acting out the Christmas story. So for their trip to Bethlehem, Joseph pulled Mary along in a little red wagon bearing a sign that said "Donkey." The shepherds in the fields wore overalls and sat around a fire while toasting marshmallows. When the angel appeared to them, she swung on a tire hanging

from a tree. The magi searched the skies through a tele-scope and rode their bikes to follow the star. At the end of the video, one by one the children declared, "That night was the best night ever. It was the best night ever!"[1]

This video retelling of the Christmas story makes me wonder about the way we tell our own faith stories. Not necessarily in a professionally produced video, or in the words and imagination of children, but in person and in our own voice. Can we be as simple and direct, as warm and authentic?

> Can we tell our stories with a touch of wonder at God's work in our lives and in the world?

When I ask new members to share their faith stories with the congregation, most initially express some reluctance. "But I'm not a public speaker." "My voice will shake." "I don't have much of a story." Such concerns are quite natural; after all, it's not easy to talk about yourself in front of two hundred or more people, and it may not be any easier in a group of fifty or even two or three. Yes, your voice might well shake, if not audibly, at least on the inside. And not everyone has a dramatic story to share.

But all of that is just fine. To quote one of my favorite pieces of writing advice from author and teacher Brenda Ueland, "Everybody is talented, original and has something important to say."[2] That's especially true when it comes to God's work in our

---

1 *The Christmas Story | Kids Perspective*, YouTube video, 4:08, December 22, 2014, Remedy Films, https://www.youtube.com/watch?v=-s56Xa_C54I.
2 Brenda Ueland, *If You Want to Write: A Book about Art, Independence, and Spirit* (Minneapolis: Graywolf Press, 1987), 3.

lives, and it's borne out in what I hear from my congregation. "I leave encouraged whenever we have personal testimonies." "I feel like I know the person now."

> Sharing faith stories has been so affirming that new members say they wish they could hear testimonies from longtime members too.

At the same time, we realize that public speaking shouldn't be a membership requirement, so new members may offer a written testimony in the bulletin instead. At first, some lamented the loss of verbal testimony, but now most seem to appreciate the written ones just as much and even save them to read again. Whether spoken or written, faith stories can nurture and encourage faith.

In Acts 22:3-21, the apostle Paul told his faith story to a crowd of people. Only it wasn't in a church setting among brothers and sisters of the Christian faith; instead, Paul faced a hostile crowd that was pressing for his arrest. What could he say in his defense? How could he communicate why he acted as he did? In response, Paul shared his story—born and raised according to the Jewish law, and persecuting the people of the Way with the support of

> Paul's testimony to the crowd is one example of a faith story told in chronological order from childhood to his present day. It's a before-and-after picture with a dramatic conversion in the middle. But not every faith story in Scripture or in real life unfolds in the same way.

the religious authorities, until one day he met Jesus. The light of the risen Christ was so bright that Paul lost his sight, and when he could see again, he was a changed man. Instead of persecuting the people of the Way, he joined them, and Christ gave him a new commission as his ambassador.

ALLAN EITZEN/MENNOMEDIA

In Acts 16:13-15, Lydia was already a God-worshiper and a woman of prayer when she heard Paul speak. For her, faith in Jesus was a deepening of the faith she already knew, and in response, she was baptized and offered hospitality to Paul and those who were traveling with him. In the early church, Timothy was a young leader who learned his faith from his grandmother Lois and his mother, Eunice (2 Timothy 1:5). Instead of experiencing a dramatic conversion like Paul, Timothy grew up in the Christian faith and came to embrace it as his own.

> [**Each faith story has a unique shape and beauty.**]

The experience of Paul is no better or worse than the experience of Lydia, and the experience of Lydia is no better or worse than the experience of Timothy. The same God was at work in each of their lives, inspiring faith and growing them in unique ways. And the same can be said of us today. Whether your faith journey is more like a seed growing secretly (Mark 4:26-29) or a sudden opening of your eyes (Mark 10:46-52), or whatever shape it might take, the same God is at work. You are God's "masterpiece" (Ephesians 2:10 *NLT*), God's work of art.

So if you get a chance to share your faith story—*when* you get a chance to share your faith story—don't be concerned that it's not interesting enough, or that it's underwhelming or overly dramatic when measured against some imaginary ideal you have in your head. Just be authentically you.

> **Wonder at God's work in your life, and allow it to shine through.**

[Talk about It]

▶ Take several moments of quiet time to think through your personal faith story. Even if you are using this study guide with a group, set aside time to reflect on your own. Have you experienced a dramatic conversion like Paul? A deepening faith like Lydia? A gradual growing up into faith like Timothy? Or is your experience completely different from theirs—are you more at the beginning of your journey? Have you experienced more ups and downs, twists and turns, back and forth?

▶ Imagine that you have been asked to share your faith story with your congregation. Instead of saying yes or no immediately, think about what you might share using the following three-part outline based on Paul's testimony in Acts 22:3-21:

> *When I was growing up (vv. 3-5):* What did faith mean to you as you were growing up? What did you learn about God from parents, church, or other sources?

> *How I came to faith (vv. 6-16):* If you had a dramatic con-
version or can identify a particular turning point in your
life, tell that part of your story. If your experience was more
gradual, share examples of how your faith became your
own, for example, who and what helped you to grow? What
role did prayer and Scripture play?

> *What my faith is like today (vv. 17-21):* How would you
describe your relationship with Jesus today? How do you
live out your faith in daily life? What Scripture and spiritual
practices nurture and sustain you?

▶ Make a list of storytelling opportunities that already exist in
your faith community, such as new member testimonies, sub-
mitting a story to the church newsletter, offering a eulogy at a
funeral, and other ideas. Then add to your list by brainstorming additional possibilities, like an intergenerational meal with
storytelling, or creating a story book for your church library.

Follow through on one of your brainstorming ideas, and share
your faith story.

3:
[Sharing Faith Stories for Every Day]

From my husband's work in narrative, I've learned that a story beginning *in media res* starts in the middle of the action. The Latin phrase literally means "in the midst of things"; so for example, the opening scene might be a rescue operation already in progress, and only later do we learn how the child managed to get trapped in the collapsed mine shaft in the first place. The middle of the action grabs our attention with its drama and intensity, and then the story gets filled in from beginning to end.

Sharing faith stories as part of everyday living also takes place **in media res**, in the middle of things. As demonstrated in last session's brainstorming, opportunities abound for the classic personal testimony that traces the journey from the beginning of faith to the present day.

> As we engage on a daily basis with family members, neighbors, friends, coworkers, and others, sharing faith stories may occur more naturally in bits and pieces as we share our lives together.

One day I went to a place new to get my hair cut. I had never met the hairdresser before, so after exchanging pleasantries about the weather and about my hair, she asked, "What do you do?" I said, "I'm a pastor." And she said, "What's that?"

We were definitely in the middle of things, as she was cutting my hair. It didn't seem appropriate to share my whole life story at that point. But answering her question was definitely a storytelling opportunity, a chance for me to share a glimpse of what it means to be a person of faith, a slice-of-life short story instead of a whole biography. So I told her about my work as a pastor to help people draw near to God—how that sometimes means praying, speaking on a Sunday morning, talking with children, or visiting someone in the hospital. I only had a few sentences before our conversation moved on to something else, and I never did get to fill in the story from the beginning. I only gave her a tiny piece of my story *in media res.*

Many faith stories appear in Scripture in a similar way, as a slice of life with little background and no well-defined ending.

Like the story of Deborah, who served the people of Israel as a prophet and judge, who helped them win their freedom from the Canaanites, and whose story abruptly ends: "And the land had rest forty years" (Judges 5:31). Or John, writing the book of Revelation and already in exile on the island of Patmos—but we are never told why or when or what happened to him (Revelation 1:9).

> We don't always hear the whole story of the people we encounter in Scripture or from the people we meet in real life, and we don't always get to share our whole story with others.

Even a partial story can communicate faith in an authentic way. It can make a real connection with someone who may have questions, and can pave the way for further conversation, further faith stories, and further steps of faith.

In John 4, Jesus shared part of his life story with a Samaritan woman. He didn't begin with the words of the prophets who anticipated his coming, or with his birth in the town of Bethlehem. Instead, he told his story in bits and pieces *in media res,* and his example suggests a few basic principles for how we might share our faith stories in the midst of everyday living.

Go where the people are. Because of the animosity between Jews and Samaritans, many Jews of Jesus' time refused to travel through Samaria, even if that refusal meant going many miles out of their way. But when Jesus left Judea to return to Galilee, he took the most direct route through Samaria. What's more, instead of avoiding people, he sat down at the well. Although he was tired and thirsty, he was also ready to talk.

Be respectful as you reach out. By striking up a conversation with the Samaritan woman who had come to the well for water, Jesus bypassed many of the social conventions of his day. As the woman herself acknowledged, Jews and Samaritans did not normally associate with one another. That was true also for rabbis and women, and men and women in general. Jesus reached across these social barriers, but he did so in a

considerate way, by doing so in a public setting and by speaking to the woman with respect.

Start with something you have in common. Both Jesus
and the woman had come to the well for water, and Jesus began their conversation with their common concern. Just as my new hairdresser and I started talking about hair, or as you might talk with a neighbor about the new community center, or with a co-worker about upcoming vacation plans. Everyday faith stories start with the everydayness of our lives.

Have an honest conversation. Jesus spoke freely and hon-
estly about his identity as the living water, as the Messiah that everyone was waiting for. But this was no one-way promotional speech. When the woman expressed confusion, he patiently responded. When she challenged him with probing questions, he answered her directly and made some good points of his own about worship, spirit, and truth.

Leave room for God's Spirit. Jesus didn't neatly wrap up
their conversation with a prayer. When Jesus' disciples arrived and the woman went into the city, she still expressed some doubts. "He cannot be the Messiah, can he?" she asked (v. 29). Yet she evidently had enough faith to tell the people about Jesus, enough that many would meet Jesus for themselves and come to believe.

[Talk about It]

▶ This session outlines five principles for sharing faith stories based on John 4. Which of these do you personally find the most challenging? What other principles or qualities can you identify: (a) in this story of Jesus and the Samaritan woman, and (b) from your own life experience?

▶ Just as Jesus shared some of his life story with the woman at the well, she went on to share some of her life story and first stirrings of faith in Jesus with the people of her town. What did she tell them, and how did they respond? Given her background and personality as illustrated in John 4, in what ways would she have made a credible witness? In what ways might they have questioned her story about Jesus?

▶ Make a list of all the people you encountered during the past week. What faith stories did you hear or did you share? Was faith a natural part of your conversation? Why or why not?

▶ Practice discerning and telling a slice-of-life faith story by asking yourself, "Where did I see God at work this week?" Think of the five W's of a good journalistic story: *Who* was involved, *what* happened and *when*, *where* did it take place, and *why*? If you're part of a group study, tell your story to one another. If you're using this material on your own, practice with a family member, friend, or fellow church member.

4:
Sharing Faith Stories in Words and Actions

In advertising, making false claims for a product can cost a company millions of dollars. Dannon settled a class action suit for $45 million when a judge ruled that its yogurt "scientifically proven" to enhance the immune system had not, in fact, been proven. New Balance paid a $2.3 million settlement for claiming that advanced shoe technology meant its sneakers would help wearers burn extra calories. Lumos Labs paid a fine of $2 million for claiming that its brain-training Lumosity games could prevent Alzheimer's disease. In each case, the story told by the advertiser did not match the reality of its product.[1]

---

1   Will Heilpern, "18 False Advertising Scandals That Cost Some Brands Millions," *Business Insider*, March 31, 2016, http://www.businessinsider.com/false-advertising-scandals-2016-3/.

Sharing faith stories isn't advertising—we're not selling anything, and no money changes hands. But as in any communication, we communicate faith stories most effectively when our words and actions reflect and reinforce one another.

> Personal stories can speak powerfully, but if our actions contradict our words, the power drains away. Actions can speak powerfully, but may also be confusing without a clear testimony in words.

During his earthly ministry, Jesus' preaching and teaching spoke so powerfully that his words even reached John the Baptist in prison. Impressed by what he heard, John sent his disciples to Jesus with this message: "Are you the one who is to come, or are we to wait for another?" **Jesus replied by pointing to his actions**, "Go and tell John what you hear and see: the blind receive their sight, the lame walk, the lepers are cleansed, the deaf hear, the dead are raised, and the poor have good news brought to them" (Matthew 11:1-5).

> For Jesus, words and actions clearly went together. He preached good news and lived it out.

In a recent funeral meditation, I shared part of the faith story of one of our church members. He and his wife prayed and read Scripture together every morning. They came to worship faithfully every Sunday. And during the week, he lived out his faith in practical ways by volunteering in the community. He always seemed to be serving on a board, fixing something for someone, or helping out in some other way. As a man of faith, he put his faith into action. As a man of action, he grounded his many activities in his faith. Words and actions combined to tell a beautiful and powerful faith story.

In the story of Zacchaeus, words and actions also work together in a beautiful and powerful way (Luke 19:1-10). From the outset, we learn that Zacchaeus was a wealthy tax collector—a "chief" tax collector, which made him even more complicit in a system hated by the people and widely thought to be corrupt, with so-called taxes lining the personal pockets of the tax collectors. No wonder Zacchaeus was wealthy.

At the same time, Zacchaeus was eager to see Jesus—so eager that he ran ahead of the crowd, so eager that he climbed a tree in order to see Jesus passing by. To his surprise, Jesus called out to him, "Zacchaeus, hurry and come down; for I must stay at

your house today" (v. 5). Zacchaeus quickly scrambled down and made arrangements, while some grumbled at the unlikely pairing. Why would an honorable teacher like Jesus visit an unscrupulous tax collector?

When Jesus arrived at his home, Zacchaeus stood before him and said, "Look, **half of my possessions**, Lord, I will give to the poor; and if I have defrauded anyone of anything, I will pay back four times as much" (v. 8). Zacchaeus's offering for the poor was much more than a token gift, much more than the tithe prescribed in the Old Testament law for poor widows and orphans (Deuteronomy 14:27-29). If that weren't already generous enough, Zacchaeus also committed himself to pay back anyone he had cheated. For voluntary restitution with remorse, the law would have required him to repay the amount he had defrauded plus 20 percent (Leviticus 6:1-7). But Zacchaeus promised to do more, with a fourfold restitution that was normally reserved only for the most extreme cases (2 Samuel 12:1-6).

In response, Jesus declared, "Today salvation has come to this house" (v. 9). Zacchaeus had demonstrated his newfound faith by hosting Jesus in his home, by showing generosity to the poor, by repenting of his previous fraudulent behavior, and by making restitution. Zacchaeus was a changed man from the chief tax collector that everyone knew, hated, and feared. **Injustice became justice**. Greed became generosity. Zacchaeus was ready to live a new life—all because of Jesus.

James 2:14-17 also reinforces the **need for faith and action**:

> What good is it, my brothers and sisters, if you say you have faith but do not have works? Can faith save you? If a brother or sister is naked and lacks daily food, and one of you says to them, "Go in peace; keep warm and eat your fill," and yet

you do not supply their bodily needs, what is the good of that? So faith by itself, if it has no works, is dead.

Church tradition tells us that these words were written by James, the half brother of Jesus, and a leader in the early church. He became known as the man with "**camel's knees**," because he would kneel to pray so often and so fervently that he developed thick calluses on both his knees. Yet as a man of faith and prayer, when James wrote his letter, he firmly connected faith and action, action and faith. One without the other was useless, and so also with stories of faith.

> Like Jesus, when we share good news,
> we need to live it out.

[Talk about It]

▶ An older church member once told me the story of an Amish man who was asked, "Are you a Christian?" and the man replied, "Ask my neighbor." Since then, I've heard variations of this story, but all make the same point. Whatever confession of faith we might say with our lips, whatever faith stories we might tell, the lives we live also tell a story. But what, then, should a neighbor be able to see as evidence of our Christian faith and identity? Second Corinthians 9:13-15 suggest that acts of generosity offer proof of faith. What other acts, behaviors, and visible signs contribute to a vibrant faith story?

▶ Reflect more deeply on the story of Zacchaeus by thinking about your own life of faith and action. In what ways do you live out your faith? In what ways do you sense tension between your Christian faith and the way you live your life? When our words and actions are at odds with one another, both our personal integrity and testimony are weakened. Have you be-haved fraudulently or unjustly like Zacchaeus? Where might God's Spirit be convicting you of a need for repentance and restitution?

▶ For a prayer of confession and repentance, read Psalm 51:1-12. Then seek to make amends by apologizing to whomever you have wronged. Repay whatever you owe by more than one to one. Be generous, for God has been generous with you. If you need help to resolve this, speak to a pastor or other trusted spiritual friend or advisor for further counsel.

▶ Brainstorm a list of practical, positive ways to share your faith story by your actions, and then choose one to follow through on. Think of random acts of kindness, volunteer opportuni-ties in your church or community, and other behaviors that demonstrate your faith.

5:
Sharing Faith Stories When It's Difficult

As detailed in the movie *Concussion*, forensic pathologist Dr. Bennet Omalu discoverd that professional football players suffered brain damage as a result of repeated blows to the head. While this pattern had previously been identified in professional boxers decades earlier, its presence among football players came as unexpected and unwelcome news. As journalist Jeanne Marie Laskas suggested, only someone like Dr. Omalu—who was originally from Nigeria and not swept up in the almost religious fervor of American football—could have made such a discovery.[1]

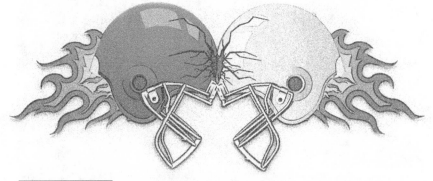

1   Suzanne Koven, "An Outsider Exposes Damaging Truth in 'Concussion,'" *Boston Globe*, November 30, 2015, https://www.bostonglobe.com/arts/2015/11/29/outsiders-expose-damaging-truth-concussion/vEWuC8YwYOZSWbeydDNwxJ/story.html.

When Dr. Omalu published his findings, he faced a wave of negative response. The National Football League demanded a retraction and refused to hear his presentation. He received threats, and his wife was followed. He was told to "go back to Africa." Yet even in the face of opposition and personal danger, he insisted on telling the truth. His persistence finally won the day as the evidence mounted, and the league had to face the reality of brain trauma among its players.

As truth telling was costly for Dr. Omalu, so sharing faith stories may also be costly. In the 16th century, Anabaptist Christians in Europe suffered persecution and death for their efforts in evangelism and telling the story of Jesus. Their testimonies communicated so powerfully that in some cases the

Anneken Hendriks, burned at Amsterdam, 1571 CE. By Jan Luyken, *Martyrs Mirror.*

authorities would carry out their executions in private, for public executions had become occasions for further evangelism and more converts.

Compared to the Anabaptists of 16th-century Europe, Christians in North America today live in relative safety. When we tell the story of Jesus or share our personal faith stories, there is no arrest warrant, no trial, no execution by hanging, burning, drowning, or other means. Yet even as I write these words, I remember that soon after I began pastoral ministry, a church member warned me about being in the building alone, because a pastor in a neighboring community had been shot while sitting in his church office. In South Carolina, nine people were shot and killed as they met for prayer in a historic black church. Such incidents are complicated by race, mental health, and other issues, but they remind me that being Christian does not mean automatically being safe.

[**Sharing faith stories means taking a risk.**]

As we share faith stories **we take a risk**, for we must face our fears, bear with uncertainty, and meet with possible criticism, misunderstanding, ridicule, and scorn. In many places around the world, Christians have also been subjected to false accusations, rape, arrest, torture, kidnapping, imprisonment, mob attacks, homelessness, bombings, beheadings, and other forms of persecution and death. For Christians enduring such trials, sharing faith stories means taking up the cross of suffering and self-sacrifice as they seek to follow Jesus (Matthew 16:24-26).

> In 2 Timothy 1:8, the apostle Paul urged Timothy: "Do not be ashamed, then, of the testimony about our Lord or of me his prisoner, but join with me in suffering for the gospel."

The apostle Paul had suffered beatings, shipwreck, hunger and thirst, sleeplessness, stoning, imprisonment, threats on his life, danger from bandits, false brothers and sisters, and perilous travel (2 Corinthians 11:24-27). He apparently wrote to Timothy from prison, as he described himself in chains (2 Timothy 1:16; 2:9).

For Timothy, a young church leader based in Ephesus, suffering for the gospel took a different form. Instead of facing the rigors of ancient travel, Timothy faced the challenge of staying in one place to give consistent leadership to the church. In the face of false teaching, he needed to admonish and instruct others (1 Timothy 1:3-11) and to set a good example (4:1-16; 6:11-19). In the face of discouragement, he needed to "rekindle the gift" that God had given him (2 Timothy 1:6), do his best (2:15), persevere (4:2), and not allow others to look down on him because of his youthfulness (1 Timothy 4:12).

Rekindle the gift of God that is within you. The faith stories of Scripture and the faith stories we live on a daily basis are gifts from God. We're meant to share our stories as wonderful

> Our challenges and risks in sharing faith stories may be quite different from those of Paul and Timothy, but their experience offers some practical direction as we seek to be faithful in our own time and place.

gifts, just as Paul and Timothy's mother and grandmother passed on their stories to Timothy, and as Timothy taught others.

Rely on God's Spirit of power, love, and self-discipline. Power without love and self-discipline can be destructive. Love without power and self-discipline can be weak. Self-discipline without power is impossible, and without love it becomes rigid and cold. But together, these three act against any spirit of fear as God empowers and works through us.

Recognize suffering as part of our calling. Just as Jesus' life and ministry meant suffering, we as his followers may also suffer. In God's upside-down kingdom, the goal in life is not necessarily to be pain free, but to be faithful. In his letter to Timothy, Paul calls this our "holy calling" (2 Timothy 1:9).

Know that you are not forgotten or alone. As we bear witness to Jesus, we are part of the body of Christ that stretches around the world and throughout history right back to Paul and Timothy. We can be part of a local congregation as a community of storytellers, and we have the privilege of praying for Christians around the world so that those who are persecuted or in prison are not forgotten.

[Talk about It]

▶ As Dr. Omalu tried to share the results of his work, he faced both personal challenges and external barriers. The personal stress for him and his wife became so great that they relocated to another city across the country. The external barriers included the negative responses from National Football League officials and players. Think of a specific instance when you faced a negative response or felt unable to share a faith story.

What did you find most difficult personally? What external barriers did you encounter? What was the result?

▶ How does God's Spirit of power, love, and self-discipline help you to deal with the challenges related to sharing faith stories? Note that love and self-discipline form part of the fruit of the Spirit in Galatians 5:22-23. How do the other fruit of the Spirit apply to the challenges of sharing faith stories? What other qualities and spiritual practices help you to share stories of faith even when it's difficult to do so?

▶ Some faith stories may be difficult to tell because they involve crises of faith, the loss of faith, experiences of sexual abuse, violence, or other trauma. A reader who looked at this man-uscript before it was printed suggests that not everyone has earned the right to hear your story, or it might not be safe to share in certain settings. What conditions make storytelling safe or unsafe? How do you balance the concern for safety with Jesus' radical call to take up your cross and follow?

▶ Observe a moment of silence in memory of Christians around the world who are imprisoned or suffering other persecution because of their stories of faith. Pray for justice, peace, and re-lief from suffering.

6:

[Sharing Faith Stories as a Community]

On the news one day, I heard about a man who had moved all his living room furniture to his front yard. No, he wasn't having a garage sale. He wasn't trying to sell his sofa and end tables. "I'm just trying to connect with my neighbors," he said. He didn't know anyone else who lived on his street. People didn't greet each other when they walked by. He felt so isolated that he came up with the novel idea of moving his living room to his front yard with the hope of finally meeting his neighbors. He wanted to create community.

As Father, Son, and Holy Spirit—Creator, Redeemer, and Sustainer—God exists in relationship, and created humanity for relationship with God and with one another (Genesis 2:4-25). God chose Abraham and Sarah to start a family that would bless "all the families of the earth" (Genesis 12:1-3). God called Moses to lead the Hebrew people out of captivity in Egypt and gave them the Ten Commandments as a guide for their life together as a community (Exodus 20:1-17). Jesus called together a band of 12 disciples and sent them out to create more community (Matthew 10:1-10). The story of the early church was the story of Christian community in Jerusalem, Corinth, Ephesus, Philippi, Rome, and beyond.

> [The story of the Bible is all about how God creates community]

Of course, the Bible tells many individual stories, but for the most part these stories are **embedded in community**. So Paul shares his personal testimony in Acts 22:3-21, but his story ends with his commission to plant new Christian communities among the Gentiles. A woman has a personal conversation with Jesus at a well in Samaria, but she immediately shares her faith story with the people of her town, who come to believe in Jesus (John 4:1-42).

Zacchaeus expresses his salvation by seeking to repair his relationships within his community (Luke 19:1-10). Lydia is part of a group of God-fearing women, and when she puts her faith in Jesus, she and her household are baptized and she insists on providing hospitality to Paul and his coworkers (Acts 16:13-15).

In these and many other examples, the individual stories are part of a larger whole.

> In fact, the emphasis in the Bible seems to fall less on telling these individual faith stories and more on how they affect the faith story of the entire community.

So we understand the significance of Abraham and Sarah only in the context of the Hebrew people as a whole. In the Jerusalem church, there must have been many individual stories, but Acts 2:43-47 tells the corporate story of the church where the apostles performed many miracles, the believers held their possessions in common, they worshiped daily in the temple, and ate together in their homes. The cumulative impact of the Christian community seemed to be greater than the sum of its parts as it spoke powerfully to the people of the city.

This biblical witness presents us with a challenge. Instead of focusing solely on sharing individual faith stories, we must also pay attention to the corporate stories that we tell as communities of faith. **What story are we telling in our corporate life** as a church? Is it a story of integrity in both words and actions? Or do we say one thing and do another? Do we share a positive witness like the Jerusalem church?

When churches and other Christian organizations look the other way in cases of abuse, when they ignore the human rights of their workers or terminate employees unjustly, when they take pride in wealth and ignore the poor, when they care more about the bottom line than about compassion for others, their story is one of failure instead of faith. *Our* story is one of failure instead of faith, for we are the church.

What we need, instead, is for our corporate story to be a positive witness like that of the Jerusalem church, which had "the goodwill of all the people" (v. 47). What if we were known for our sincere and steady worship of God as they were known among the people? What if we could care for one another with respect and compassion? What if we could practice hospitality and generosity as they did? That's the faith story I would love to be a part of and share with others.

In 2 Corinthians 8:1-7, the apostle Paul shares a story about the churches in Macedonia. These congregations lived in "extreme poverty," but when they heard of how other Christians were struggling and needed help, they begged to offer their assistance and gave generously out of what little they had. Even more importantly, they first gave of themselves to God and to Paul and his coworkers. Like the church in Jerusalem, the churches of Macedonia seemed to have their priorities straight.

Paul tells this story to encourage the church of Corinth that they too might give priority to supporting Christians who were struggling. We might suspect him of guilting them into giving generously, although he is quick to say that he is not making any demands on them. Yet he can't help but point out that in contrast to the churches of Macedonia, the church of Corinth has an abundance that could help meet the need of others "in order that there might be a fair balance" (v. 14).

> What faith stories might we share with one another as churches today? Do we have stories of worship, of caring for one another, of generosity? How can we encourage one another within the body of Christ and also reach out to others by sharing our faith stories?

[Talk about It]

▶ Acts 2:43-47 tells the faith story of the Jerusalem church in just a few sentences by highlighting some key activities (e.g., worship, eating in homes) and characteristics (e.g., caring, generosity). What key practices and characteristics would sum up your congregation's faith story?

▶ Another way to share our corporate faith story is to share a slice of our life story *in media res*, in the midst of things. Where do you see God at work in the midst of your congregation? What good news story from your life as a church would encourage other churches? Where and how could you share that story?

▶ As you consider the corporate faith story and witness of the church, what parts to do you find difficult or problematic? Where do you see a need for confession, repentance, and restoration? What attitudes and behaviors need to change? How can we receive God's forgiveness and new life and go on to tell a better corporate faith story with integrity in our words and actions?

▶ As you conclude this study, give thanks for the power of story to communicate God's good news, to draw people to Jesus, and to create community. Reflect again on your personal story and how it connects to the larger, corporate faith story of the church. Pray for God's grace, wisdom, love, and power to share and live out our faith stories in ways that honor God and respect other people. May God's story continue to be written in our lives, and may we respond with faith, hope, and love. "Grace, mercy, and peace from God the Father and Christ Jesus our Lord" (1 Timothy 1:2).

[About the Writer]

April Yamasaki loves stories in her preaching, writing, and daily life. Whether she's preparing a sermon, writing an article, watching a movie with her husband, or visiting with someone over tea, she's experienced the unique power of stories to express faith in ways that draw people toward God and to one another. That's what drew her to this Bible study on sharing faith stories.

As the lead pastor of Emmanuel Mennonite Church in Abbotsford, British Columbia, April is fully engaged in the church's story of following Jesus, being community minded, and having a global perspective. She is a catalyst and encourager to engage people in using their gifts, and enjoys expressing her creativity and love of Scripture in worship and preaching.

Beyond her pastoral work, April is the author of *Christ Is for Us: A Lenten Study Based on the Revised Common Lectionary*; *Spark: Igniting Your God-Given Creativity*; *Sacred Pauses: Spiritual Practices for Personal Renewal*; *Ordinary Time with Jesus*; and other books on Christian living. Her writing has appeared in print and online in numerous places, including the *Christian Century, Canadian Mennonite, Redbud Post,* and *Rejoice!*

April keeps in touch with readers and shares faith-focused and writing-related stories on her main website, Writing and Other Acts of Faith (aprilyamasaki.com). She also curates a blog on

employment practices in the church and other Christian organizations called When You Work for the Church: The Good, the
Bad, and the Ugly and How We Can All Do Better
(whenyouworkforthechurch.com).

A third-generation Canadian of Chinese descent, April was
born and raised in Vancouver, British Columbia, earned a mas-
ter's degree in Christian studies, and has taught college-level
courses in Bible and English, continuing education courses on
spiritual practice, as well as seminars and retreats. She lives in
Abbotsford with her husband, Gary.